D0801874

DON'TS
FOR HUSBANDS

DON'TS
FOR HUSBANDS

BY

BLANCHE EBBUTT

LONDON
A. & C. BLACK, LTD.
1913

PREFACE

My dear Sir,

You are neither as bad nor as good a fellow as you imagine yourself to be. No doubt you know a good deal about women, but (if you are in the early years of your married life) not nearly as much as you will in another decade. In any case I hope that, when you have read my little book, you will thank me for having told you many things that otherwise you could have learned only by experience, more or less bitter according to the discretion exercised both by you and by your other half.

Women, married or single, are kittle-cattle; and, as for men—well, I have a husband myself!

BLANCHE EBBUTT.

DON'TS FOR HUSBANDS

I.—GENERAL HABITS.

DON'T drop cigarette ash all over the drawing-room carpet. Some people will tell you that it improves the colours, but your wife won't care to try that recipe.

Don't throw cigar-ends into the bowl of water your wife keeps in front of the gas-fire. They are not ornamental, and she will not be pleased.

Don't increase the necessary work of the house by leaving all your things lying about in different places. If you are not tidy by nature, at least be thoughtful for others.

Don't sit down to breakfast in your shirt-sleeves in hot weather on the ground that "only your wife" is present. She is a woman like any other woman. The courtesies you give to womankind are her due, and she will appreciate them.

Don't take it out on your poor wife every time you have a headache or a cold. It isn't her fault, and she has enough to do in nursing you, without having to put up with ill-humour into the bargain.

Don't flourish a grimy handkerchief about because you have forgotten to take a clean one out of your box or your drawer. If your wife provides you with a reasonable stock, you might at least take the trouble to remember to use them.

Don't stoop, even if your work is desk-work. Your wife wants to see you straight and broad-chested.

Don't slouch. No one who cares for a man likes to see him acquire a slouching habit.

Don't be too grave and solemn. Raise a bit of fun in the home now and then.

Don't keep all your best jokes for your men friends. Let your wife share them.

Don't look at things solely from a man's point of view. Put yourself in your wife's place and see how you would like some of the things she has to put up with.

Don't fidget. Some husbands are never still for a moment. They walk in and out of rooms like the wandering Jew; they play with the salt at dinner; they draw lines on the table-cloth with a fork; they tap the table with their fingers and the floor with their feet; they creak their slippers and drop the coal tongs on to the tiled hearth. In fact, they keep their wives in a state of tension, and the poor creatures would need nerves of iron to enable them to stand the strain.

Don't make a fuss when your wife has "unattached" women friends to be seen home at night. I have seen men on these occasions look at their slippers, and fuss about changing into walking-shoes, and look out to see whether it rains, etc., until I should certainly have gone off alone had I been the guest to be escorted.

Don't sharpen pencils all over the house as you walk about. Try a hearth or a waste-paper basket, or a newspaper. It does not improve either carpets or the servants' temper to find scraps of pencil-sharpenings all over the floors.

Don't delegate the carving to your wife on the plea that you "can't" carve. You should be ashamed to own that you can't do a little thing like that as well as a woman can. It is just laziness on your part. Besides, a man ought to take the head of his own table.

Don't always refuse to go shopping with your wife. Of course it's a nuisance, but sometimes she honestly wants your advice, and you ought to be pleased to give it.

Don't be conceited about your good looks. It is more than probable that no one but yourself is aware of them ; anyway, you are not responsible for them, and vanity in a man is ridiculous.

Don't refuse to get up and investigate in the night if your wife hears an unusual noise, or fancies she smells fire or escaping gas. She will be afraid of shaming you by getting up herself, and will lie awake working herself into a fever. This may be illogical, but it's true.

Don't hang about the house all day if your occupation does not take you abroad. Spend regular hours in your study or "den," or go out and play golf; but don't inflict your company on your wife during every minute of every day. She is fond of you, but she wants to be free sometimes. And *she* has business to do, if you haven't.

II.—PERSONAL RELATIONS.

Don't keep up the "poor little woman" pose too long. A woman may like to be a plaything for a little while, but the novelty soon wears off.

Don't condescend; you are not the only person in the house with brains.

Don't be surprised, or annoyed, or disappointed, to find, after treating your wife for years as a feather-brain, that you have made her one, and that she fails to rise to the occasion when you need her help.

Don't keep her in cotton-wool. She isn't wax—she's a woman.

Don't try to take all work and worry off her shoulders. You can't attend to her business and your own too.

Don't shelter her from every wind that blows. You will kill her soul that way, if you save her body.

Don't forget that you are not immortal. What chance will she have if you die and leave her with no knowledge of the ways of the wicked world?

Don't omit to bring home an occasional bunch of flowers or a few chocolates. Your wife will value even a penny bunch of violets for your thought of her.

Don't rush out of the house in such a hurry that you haven't time to kiss your wife "good-bye." She will grieve over the omission all day.

Don't belittle your wife before visitors. You may think it a joke to speak of her little foibles, but she will not easily forgive you.

Don't be careless about keeping promises made to your wife. If you have promised to be at home at seven, think twice before you go off with a friend at 6.30.

Don't hesitate to mention the fact when you think your wife looks especially nice. Your thinking so can give her no pleasure unless you tell your thought.

Don't forget your wife's birthday. Even if she doesn't want the whole world to know her age, she doesn't like *you* to forget.

Don't think that because you can't afford to buy an expensive present, it is best to take no notice at all. The smallest gift will be appreciated if prompted by love.

Don't sulk when things go wrong. If you can't help being vexed, say so, and get it over.

Don't "nag" your wife. If she *has* burnt the cake or forgotten to sew on a button, she doesn't want to be told of it over and over again.

Don't shout when you are angry. It isn't necessary to let the children or the servants know all about it.

Don't scowl or look severe. Cultivate a pleasant expression if Nature hasn't blessed you with one.

Don't "let off steam" on your wife or children every time anything goes wrong in the garage or the garden, or the fowl-house, or the dark room.

Try to realise that they have nothing to do with it, and that it is unfair to make them suffer for it.

Don't allow yourself to become selfish. It is so easy, because wives are mostly ready to give way. Watch yourself, and if you find that you always tend to appropriate the most comfortable chair, or the warmest corner, or the most interesting book, just check the habit.

Don't quarrel with your wife. She can't, if you won't. Mud sticks, and so do words spoken in anger.

Don't refuse your wife's overtures when next you meet if you *have* unfortunately had a bit of a breeze. Remember it costs her something to make them, and if you weren't a bit of a pig, you would save her the embarrassment by making them yourself.

Don't ever tell your wife a lie about anything. There should be entire confidence between you. If she once finds you out in a lie, she will not believe you when you *do* speak the truth.

Don't "talk down" to your wife. She has as much intelligence as your colleague at the office; she lacks only opportunity. Talk to her (explaining when necessary) of anything you would talk of to a man, and you will be surprised to find how she expands.

Don't think that it is no longer necessary to *show* your love for your wife, as she "ought to know it by this time." A woman likes to be kissed and caressed and to receive little lover-like attentions from her husband even when she is a grandmother.

Don't expect happiness if you married for money; once she realises it, your wife won't let you forget it.

Don't think that if you married merely to get an unpaid housekeeper that position is going to satisfy your wife. She could have obtained a good salary as professional housekeeper to any other man if she had wanted to: she married for other reasons.

Don't think that because you and your wife married for love there will never be a cloud in your sky. Neither of you is perfect, and you will have to learn to avoid treading on each other's corns.

Don't expect your wife to do all the cheering up while you do all the giving way when things go wrong. Share and share alike.

Don't dwell on any lack of physical perfection in your wife. Beauty of mind is much more important than beauty of body.

Don't despise your wife's everyday qualities because she is not what the world would call brilliant. Sound common sense is of more value than fireworks when one is running a home.

Don't call your wife a coward because she is afraid of a spider. Probably in a case of real danger she would prove to be quite as brave as you.

Don't be irritated now by the childish ways in your wife that amused you so much in your *fiancée*. She will grow out of them soon enough.

Don't put on too much of the "lord of creation" air. It will only make you look ridiculous.

Don't think that, because she is a woman, your wife ought to be an angel of light. She is just as much a human being as you are, and no more perfect.

Don't keep your wife outside your business interests. It is foolish to say that she knows nothing about the business, and therefore it can't interest her.

You will often find, too, that her fresh mind will see a way out of some little difficulty that has not occurred to you.

Don't worship your wife as a saint, and then when you discover that she is, after all, of common clay, spend the rest of your life mourning her deterioration. Probably she is what she always was, and it is only that you are looking at her through different glasses.

Don't take the attitude that wives, like children, should be seen and not heard. No doubt you are a very clever fellow, and it is an education for her to listen to you, but she also may have some views worth mentioning.

Don't expect to understand every detail of the working of your wife's mind. A woman arrives at things by different ways, and it is useless to worry her with "Why?" does she think this or that.

Don't try to keep bad news from your wife. She will guess that something is wrong, and will worry far more than if you tell her straight out.

Don't neglect seeing your wife off, or meeting her on her return from a journey, on the ground that she is so capable that she doesn't need you. Perhaps not, but she would like to see you, all the same.

Don't allow the habit of silence at home to grow upon you. Of course, you don't want to keep up polite conversation with an effort—that is not at all what I mean; but some husbands never seem to think it worth while to talk to their wives about anything, although if a friend comes in, they will at once begin an animated conversation.

Don't expect your wife to wait on you hand and foot. She is good for other things than to fetch and carry for you. If you don't exact it, it will give her pleasure to wait on you to a reasonable extent.

Don't think you can live your lives apart under the same roof and still be happy. Marriage is a joint affair, and cannot comfortably be worked along separate lines.

Don't insist upon having the last word. If you know when to drop an argument, you are a wise man.

Don't think it is undignified to give way where you and your wife think differently. If it is on a matter of principle, show her why you think as you do, and she will respect your reasons; but you must equally hear her reasons and respect them.

Don't try to regulate every detail of your wife's life. Even a wife is an Individual, and must be allowed some scope.

Don't expect your wife to hold the same views as yours on every conceivable question. Some men like an echo, it is true, but it becomes very wearisome in time.

Don't hesitate to talk politics with your wife. Many men are satisfied to believe that "women don't understand politics." Why don't they? Because they never have a chance to crystallise their beliefs by thrashing out questions of public interest in argument with men who have studied them. Encourage your wife to read and talk of political matters. Never mind if she sees things quite differently from you; let her form her own views and express them.

Don't drop, when alone with your wife, the little courtesies you would offer to other women. For instance, always get up to open a door for her, as you would for a lady guest.

Don't fall into the habit of regarding your wife merely as the mother of your children. There is no need for her to cease to be your chum because she is a mother; but if she finds that you tend to relegate her to a back seat, she will gradually allow the children to absorb her more and more.

Don't drop calling her "Laura" or "Kiddie," and address her as "Mamma" or "Mother" in season and out of season. She is proud to be a mother, but she wants to be a wife too.

Don't try to "drive" your wife. You will find it so much easier to lead her.

Don't be "riled" by a bit of good-natured chaff from your wife. There is no bitterness in it, and she probably has to stand a good deal of the same sort of thing from you.

Don't fail to treat your wife with due respect. Let there be nothing of the high and mighty suggestion that a mere woman can't possibly understand things. There are even realms in which you can look up to her as owning superior knowledge, and there are none in which she is to be despised.

Don't begin your married life by expecting too much. If you expect little, you will be saved a good deal of disappointment.

Don't say it's a good thing to speak home truths now and again to your wife. It only means that you want to be nasty.

Don't forget to be your wife's best friend as well as her husband. True friendship in marriage does away with all sorts of trouble.

Don't expect a "return" for every generous action. It ceases to be generous if there be an *arrière pensée* in it.

Don't chide your wife in public, whatever you may feel it necessary to do in private. She will not easily forgive you for having witnesses to her discomfiture.

Don't be chary of your praise. Whether it be a new design for a dress, a more becoming style of hairdressing, or a "fetching" little entrée at dinner, give praise where praise is due. It will not only make your wife happier, but will even confirm your own good-humour; and good-humour is always worth cultivating for its own sake.

Don't forget that actions speak louder than words. It's no use telling your wife how much you care for her if you do the very things that you know will make her unhappy.

Don't flatter your wife. Unless she is very vain, she is sure to see through you, and she will be more hurt than pleased. Praise where you can, but leave flattery alone.

Don't assume that it is always your wife who is wrong whenever you have

a difference of opinion. After all, you
are not infallible.

Don't judge your wife's motives.
She may do a thing from a motive
that would never occur to you, and be
perfectly justified in her action.

Don't be reserved with your wife,
however natural it is to you to be
reserved with others.   Be perfectly
open and confiding in all your deal-
ings with her.   She will be deeply
hurt if she is left to discover for herself something that she had a right to
expect you to tell her.

Don't let ambition crowd out love.
There ought to be room for both in
your life, but some men are so busy

"getting on" that they have no time to make love to their wives.

Don't neglect to write daily to your wife when you are absent from each other. Even if you can manage only a few lines, it will show her that you are thinking about her.

Don't think you can soothe wounded feelings by material gifts. I knew a man who bought his wife a ring or a pendant to "make it up" every time he had been especially horrid to her, but it did not heal the breach. She would gladly have given all her jewellery to feel that her husband loved her too well to hurt her.

Don't start arguments about religion unless you and your wife can both

discuss the matter quite impersonally.
The bitterest quarrels sometimes arise
from religious discussion. On the other
hand—

Don't stifle discussion in your home.
Let every member of the family
contribute his ideas, and there will
be none of the stagnation one so
often meets in homes where discussion of any and every subject is pro-
hibited.

Don't make fun of your wife if she
happens to make a little mistake. She
is probably very sensitive, and will get
into the habit of withdrawing into
her shell, so that you will lose much
valuable intercourse that might have
been yours.

Don't forget that it is the little things that count in married life. Avoid trivial jealousies; trivial selfishnesses; tiny irritants; small outbursts of temper; short sarcastic comments. If you can't say something pleasant, learn to keep silence.

III.—JEALOUSY.

Don't try to be a Sultan. This is the West; and you can't shut your wife away from other men. Don't insult her by trying to.

Don't tease your wife about every pretty girl you meet. She may not be jealous to begin with, but after a while she may begin to think that there is something in it.

Don't object to a servant on the score of her looks. You wife will take care not to engage a pretty maid if she suspects you of undue interest in her appearance.

Don't object to your wife going out with another man if you can't take her yourself—so long as you know and approve of the man.

Don't imagine your wife never wants to see any other man than you. However nice she thinks you, it is possible to have too much of a good thing.

Don't, if you think your wife sees too much of another man, forbid her to speak to him. You will perhaps only crystallise a wandering fancy by this method. Fill up her time yourself; take her out a good deal, and the too friendly attitude will soon die a natural death. But a woman of spirit won't be coerced.

Don't dwell on the beauty of other women if you know your wife to be sensitive on the point. There is no sense in rubbing sores, although some men seem to find a strange pleasure in it.

Don't be continually telling your wife what a charming woman Mrs. Jones is, or how lucky Brown is in having a wife who can cook such dainty dishes. You can't expect her to relish having the good qualities of these other wives rammed down her throat.

Don't throw your mother's perfections at her head, or you needn't be surprised if she suggests that you might as well return to your mother's wing. Remember that your mother was an experienced housekeeper before you were born, and that your wife is only just beginning.

Don't be jealous of your wife's girl friends. If she wants to spend the day with them now and then, spare her with a good grace. Don't let her feel that you are a selfish tyrant.

Don't give up all the friends of your bachelorhood. Ask them to your home, and your wife will make them welcome, whether men or women.

Don't flirt with other women. Your wife may or may not be jealous, but she will certainly despise you if you do.

Don't neglect your wife because your grown-up daughter is such a charming companion. She can be a good chum to you without usurping her mother's place in your affections.

Don't raise objections to your wife's work among the poor on the score that "charity begins at home." Quite true, but it needn't end there. It is mean of you to be jealous of the time a good woman spends in helping those less fortunate than herself.

Don't forget to trust your wife in everything—in money matters; in her relations with other men; in her correspondence. Trust her to the utmost, and you will rarely find your trust misplaced.

IV.—HINTS ON FINANCE.

Don't neglect to insure your life for a reasonable sum. Then you will at least know that your wife will not be left in actual want if you die suddenly.

Don't do all the ordering and all the paying yourself on the ground that your wife doesn't understand money matters. Let her learn to understand them.

Don't be niggardly about the household supplies if you can afford to be generous. You can't make omelettes without breaking eggs, and you can't have cheerful fires without using coal or wood pretty freely.

Don't let your wife pledge your credit beyond what is necessary and reasonable. She must learn to cut her coat according to her cloth.

Don't think your wife cares for nothing but money. Money doesn't make happiness, but the lack of it can cause a good deal of misery. When your views and hers on money matters conflict, think what a lot she has to do with her share of the family income.

Don't dole out money for your wife's personal use in sixpences on the ground that, as you pay the bills, she can't really require any money. It is hateful to a woman to have to ask for what should be hers by right.

Don't try to live on too big a scale, and don't let your wife persuade you into it against your better judgment.

Don't take a bigger house than you need just for show. You will find it will need more servants, more furniture, more everything, and you will have to scrape to keep up appearances, instead of being comfortable on a less expensive plane.

Don't live on the edge of your income while leading your wife to suppose that you have plenty of money. If she doesn't know the financial situation, she can't act for the best.

Don't spend the best years of your life in thinking of nothing but money-getting. Enjoy your life to the full with your wife and children, and relegate money-getting to its proper place —necessarily an important one, but not the only thing to be thought of.

Don't let all the economising be on your wife's side. Perhaps you could do with a little less tobacco, or fewer cigars or cigarettes, or fewer taxis, if you tried.

Don't persuade your wife to hand over to you for investment any money she may have of her own. Your intentions are the best in the world, but she will find it difficult not to hold you responsible if the investments prove to be unsatisfactory. Keep clear of her private income.

Don't get her to put her private money into your bank, "as it is the same thing." Let her keep a separate bank account, and then she will know just where she is, and be able to do as she likes with her own.

Don't ever let yourself think that marriage has spoilt your career—that if you had had no wife and children to provide for, you could have done so differently. Think rather of the happiness you would have missed that has been yours all these years.

Don't be ungracious when your wife lavishes her private money on you. It takes a strong man to receive favours

readily; if you really care for your
wife, you will let her do things for
you occasionally, and accept her offer-
ings graciously.

V.—HOUSEHOLD MATTERS.

Don't interfere with your wife's
household management. Nothing up-
sets servants more than interference in
matters of detail from the master of
the house.

Don't forget to be master in your
own house, but see that your wife is
mistress.

Don't sneer at your wife's cookery,
or bridge-playing, or singing, or, in
fact, at anything that she does. If

you do, you may raise an animosity you cannot easily allay.

Don't make up your mind to a mother-in-law difficulty. If you take her the right way, you will probably find your mother-in-law not only a charming woman, but one of your best friends.

Don't domineer over the servants. Unwilling service is never good, and a kind word or a pleasant smile will do wonders in the way of saving your wife from being harassed.

Don't run away with the idea that there is nothing to do in a house, and that your wife should therefore never be busy or tired. You work for a few hours at the office, and come right away from it until next day; but a woman's work is never done until bedtime, and then she lies awake and thinks of something she has left undone.

Don't grumble day after day at your wife's untidiness if you happen to be a methodical man. It will be much easier, and will save friction, if you quietly put away the things she leaves lying about. Her untidiness may be a constitutional defect, and, if so, no amount of grumbling will cure it.

Don't argue that no wife need be dull at home because there's always plenty to do. Of course there is; it is just the deadly monotony of it that some natures can't stand.

Don't let your wife feel that there isn't a corner of the house she can call her own. If there is only one "den," let her have half of it, or at least a roll-top desk or a bureau for her special use.

Don't be unsympathetic if your wife's worries seem to you to be trivial. You haven't tried to run a house with tiresome servants and ailing children, and you don't realise what a strain it is at times, and how molehills become mountains, because there are so many of them piled on to each other. You can soon sweep all the trouble away with a little kindly sympathy, or you can make it worse by refusing to see that there *is* any trouble.

Don't think your business worries are ever so much more important. The others are *her* business worries, and just as real to her as yours are to you.

Don't be persuaded, even if you are unfortunately childless, or if your children have married, to give up your home and live in hotels or boarding-houses. All the mechanical conveniences and perfect service won't make up for the loss of your own home. With all its imperfections, it is *yours*, and you can do as you like in it.

Don't be afraid of lending a hand in the house during a temporary servant difficulty, or if you keep no servant. It will do you no harm at all to learn to light a fire or clean a pair of boots, and be sure your wife will have to do plenty of things that *she* is unaccustomed to.

Don't let your wife become merely a domestic machine. If she doesn't want to broaden her horizon, see that you do it for her. But probably she only wants a little encouragement to lift herself out of the everlasting groove.

Don't show your worst side at home. You need to be well thought of by your wife and children even more than by strangers. You spend hours only with outsiders, but you spend your life with your family, and it depends on your conduct whether they make you happy or wretched. Let them have the benefit of your best qualities.

Don't be too didactic in your home. Your wife is not to be treated as a schoolgirl to have the law laid down by you.

Don't forget that character is more important than genius. If your wife is a true woman, don't worry about the rest.

Don't omit to cultivate a sense of humour. It will carry you safely past many a danger-signal in the home.

VI.—RECREATION AND HOLIDAYS.

Don't selfishly refuse to go out in the evening because you have been amongst other people all day. Remember that your wife hasn't, and a change is good for her.

Don't grudge an occasional evening at the theatre. If you spring it on her as a pleasant surprise, your wife will be all the more delighted.

Don't spend night after night at your club, leaving your wife alone to count the hours until your return.

Don't say she needn't stay up for you. You know quite well that she can't sleep until you are safe at home.

Don't insist on her always being home when you come in. She will like to be there to receive you as often as she can, but if you try to make a rule of it, she will consider it a grievance.

Don't take it for granted that your wife has too much to attend to now there are children to be able to go out with you as she used to do in the earlier days of your life together. Ask her; not perfunctorily, but as if you really want her, and she will generally manage to go.

Don't spring it on your wife five minutes before it is time to start that you are going to the other end of Europe, and would like her to go too. It is all very well to say that it doesn't take long to pack a couple of bags, but sometimes the things are not ready for packing. Besides, your wife has to make arrangements about the house and children which can't always be made at a moment's notice.

Don't think that you have of necessity done with walking or cycling tours now you are married, as you can't leave your wife and go away with your old chum. Why not take *her*? If you will moderate your ardour, and be content to walk fifteen miles a day instead of twenty, and to carry a slightly larger knapsack (you'll never feel the difference), you and your wife can have the most delightful walking tours together. Or if she cycles, and you will think less of the miles you cover than the charming villages you investigate, you will not need a better chum than she can be.

Don't refuse to play tennis or croquet or billiards with your wife because it is "not worth while" to play games with a woman. If she plays badly, show her how to improve. She certainly won't play better by being left out of the game altogether.

Don't tell your wife she is wasting her time if she plays games occasionally while you are at the office. It is the best way to keep her fit, and she needs a change from the monotony of the house.

Don't say it is no fun to go out cycling with your wife because she can't "scorch." It will do you no harm to ride more slowly than usual, and your company will give her a great deal of pleasure. Her "going slow" is one of the secrets of her chances of longer life. Take her with you, and you will avoid that overtaxing of the arteries which leads to premature old age.

Don't be nervous about your wife. She can take care of herself much better than you imagine, and she hates you to be fussy.

Don't settle down into an "old married man" while you are still in the prime of life. Take your wife out and about; give parties; visit your friends; and you will keep much younger than if you settle into the smoking-jacket and slippers habit.

Don't say your wife wastes time in reading, even if she reads only fiction. Help her to choose *good* fiction, and let her forget her little worries for an hour occasionally in reading of the lives of others. But, above all things, don't put on the schoolmaster air. She'll never stand that. Rather let her pick her reading for herself.

Don't discourage her if she wants to take up serious reading, even if *you* are not interested in it. Tastes differ, and you needn't call her a blue-stocking because she prefers not to be an ignoramus.

Don't say that other women find fancy needlework a sufficient relaxation. If your wife *doesn't*, why should she waste her time on that instead of going out or doing things that she *does* find recreative?

Don't say it will be holiday enough to stay at home, and spend time on your hobby instead of going to town every day for business. Remember that your wife gets no change that way (except a little extra trouble in house-keeping), and that she needs one quite as much as you do.

Don't rush off on a Continental tour, and come back worn out to be nursed up by your wife. That sort of holiday is worse than useless. Go abroad if you like, but don't spend all your time rushing from place to place sight-seeing.

Don't take a house for your summer holiday, unless your family is so large that you are obliged to. It is no holiday for your wife to have to do her housekeeping—and probably under less convenient conditions—in another town or village. If you must do it for the sake of the children, take her away to a boarding-house or hotel at another time to give her a complete holiday.

Don't insist on giving holidays to the servants during *your* holiday on the ground that your wife can "manage" at the seaside. You are not the only person to be considered, and it's no holiday for her to be tied to the children day in and day out while you go golfing or fishing. Probably *she* would like to golf or fish as well if she got the chance.

Don't growl every time your wife invites anyone to the house. It takes quite half her pleasure away to know that you think it's a "nuisance" having people about. It's bad for you too; nothing is more insidious and more ageing than the hermit habit.

Don't omit to learn to dance as soon as you get married, if your education has been neglected before. Your wife will lose half her pleasures if you can't dance.

VII.—HEALTH.

Don't be impatient if your wife has a headache, or neuralgia, or other ailment. Just because *your* health is perfect, you need not be unsympathetic. But, on the other hand—

Don't pet your wife when her little finger aches until she imagines herself a martyr to ill-health, when there is really nothing the matter with her.

Don't encourage her to be hysterical. You need not be unkind, but you can firmly refuse to pity her.

Don't let your wife become deadly ill before you insist on her seeing a doctor. Some women imagine they are ill, but others never mention it until they are at the last gasp, and *their* husbands should keep their eyes open.

Don't stubbornly refuse to put on your overcoat on a threatening morning, and then when, after getting wet through on the way to the station and sitting in your wet clothes, you develop a bad cold, take it out of your wife by being crotchety and irritable.

Don't insist on your cold dip when you don't feel fit, and then go about all day feeling shivery and miserable.

Don't shut all the windows on the ground that you can't stand draughts, and then complain of a headache.

Don't be too sensitive about your personal appearance to wear glasses if your sight requires them, and if your nose is not the right shape for pince-nez, be satisfied to wear spectacles.

Don't be continually worrying about your health. If you really feel ill, or suspect that anything is wrong, consult a doctor, instead of causing your wife untold anxiety by throwing out vague suggestions as to what "may" be the matter with you.

Don't sit up after midnight regularly, and then get up at the last minute next morning because you don't feel very fit. Get a proper night's rest.

Don't burn the candle at both ends, either as regards work or play. You won't be able to stand it for long.

VIII.—DRESS.

Don't grudge your wife a new dress because *you* haven't noticed that she needs one. You don't know how much trouble she has taken to try and appear —to other people—as if she *didn't* need one; but *she* knows.

Don't argue that a new hat isn't necessary because there is nothing visibly wrong with the one she is wearing. You have probably forgotten that this is its third season, but *she* hasn't.

Don't forget to buy your wife a pair of gloves occasionally. She will always be pleased to have them.

Don't insist on wearing your hair or your moustache in a style you know she hates. Just try it another way to please her.

Don't persist in wearing that very disreputable coat when some rather "starchy" people are coming to tea. If your wearing it makes your wife feel uncomfortable, it won't do you any harm to change it, even if you do think it a bore.

Don't growl when your wife asks you to fasten her dress up the back. You know you consider it a very becoming dress, and it would be spoilt by fastening in front.

Don't dress carelessly when you are past your first youth. All the more reason to make yourself look as nice as possible to counteract the effect of advancing years.

Don't be so absent-minded as to dress yourself "anyhow." Perhaps in the rush to get you off in time for your train, your wife may not notice that you are wearing odd socks; but she will be very uncomfortably conscious of it when she sees you again in the evening, and wonders how many people have happened to observe it during the day. She does her best, but you can't expect her actually to dress you.

Don't refuse to listen to your wife's suggestions on matters of dress. Sometimes women know what suits men better than the men themselves.

Don't try to dress your wife in the fashions of ten years ago. Some men can never like anything newer than that; but a woman does not want to look as if she came out of the ark.

Don't, if your wife is obviously cut out for a "one-piece" collarless dress and a floppy hat, persuade her to wear a "neat" black coat and skirt, high linen collars, and sailor hat, to please your ideas of decorum. She doesn't want to dress like a nursery governess.

Don't take so little interest in your wife's dress that she might as well wear a piece of old sacking as far as you are concerned. It is very discouraging to a woman to find that her husband neither knows nor cares how she dresses.

IX.—HOBBIES.

Don't spend all your money on the garden because that is *your* hobby, and leave none for the house if that happens to be your wife's hobby.

Don't omit to have a hobby of some kind. It will take you out of your wife's way when she is busy or you are cross, and you will feel a different man in half an hour.

Don't separate your pursuits from your wife's more than is necessary. Do your gardening together; work, talk, and plan together, and you will become truer comrades every year.

Don't say a married woman doesn't want to go back to school because your wife wishes to attend language classes or lectures, or to take lessons in singing or dancing. Let her do any or all of these things, and be thankful she finds so much to interest her. She will be a much brighter companion than the stick-at-home wife.

Don't give up cricket, or football, or tennis, or rowing, or whatever outdoor sport you have been accustomed to, just because you are married. Athletics will keep you from becoming flabby.

Of course, if you can get all the exercise you need in a game which your wife can share, so much the better; if not, she is not so selfish as to wish to deprive you of healthy recreation. But remember your responsibilities. Don't overdo it.

Don't expect to have a hobby in which you get the enjoyment while your wife does the hard work. If you profess to like gardening, don't tie up a rose here and there while your wife does all the hard weeding; if poultry-keeping is your hobby, don't expect her to do all the feeding, and the letting out and in of the birds; if photography, don't confine *your* work to the taking of snapshots, leaving her to do the developing and printing while you take the credit.

Don't leave your wife to clean and put away all the tools you use in gardening or carpentering. The workman should care for his own tools.

Don't "put your foot down" if your wife wants to join some society of which you don't approve. Produce your arguments; then, if she fails to find them convincing, let her be an "ist" or an "anti" to her heart's content. She really has as much right to her own opinions as you have, and there is no cause for quarrel.

Don't try to control your wife's church-going or non-church-going tendencies. The question is for her alone to decide, and you should leave her entirely free, whatever your own views may be.

Don't let any hobby so overmaster you that you spend every minute on it when you are at home, especially if it be something in which your wife can take no part. Leave *some* time to devote to her.

Don't, if music be your hobby, practise the violin, 'cello, flute, trombone, or whatever musical instrument you happen to fancy, in the drawing-room for many hours a day. Your wife may also be fond of music, and it is not fair to victimise her to this extent. She won't be able to concentrate on a book while her ear is tortured by false notes. Do your real "practising" up at the top of the house, and play for her pleasure in the drawing-room.

Don't forget to use a reasonable amount of caution should your hobby be one that may be dangerous. Your wife doesn't want you to be "funky," but she has a right to expect you not to take undue risks in your motor-car, bicycle, or flying-machine.

X.—FOOD.

Don't keep up a continual grumble at meal-times, until your wife begins to think she can never please you. She will leave off trying after a while, and your last state will be worse than your first.

Don't be too exacting about your food. If you can't afford an accomplished cook, don't demand elaborate dishes. If you do, it will mean either that your wife will spend most of her time on them, and sit down hot and tired, and perhaps cross, or the cook will spoil them; and in either case there is likely to be discord.

Don't come in at any odd time, and expect to find your dinner done to a turn. If it was ready at the time you *said* you were coming, it can't be quite as nice an hour or two later. Your home is neither a club nor an hotel.

Don't get up too late to eat a decent breakfast before starting out for your day's work. It is bad for you to go without, and will worry your wife.

Don't insist on eating indigestible things because you like them, and then blame your wife's cookery when your liver makes itself felt.

Don't let your wife feel that your dinner is the be-all and end-all of your existence.   Enjoy your food by all means, but don't make a fetish of it.

Don't refuse to eat cold meat at luncheon once in a way if you are home to that meal.   Unless you keep a large staff or domestics, or unless your small staff or your wife is very much overworked and "rushed," you can't always have a hot meal both at midday and in the evening.

Don't insist on having gorgonzola or other strong-smelling cheese on the table or the sideboard twice a day when you know the odour makes your wife feel ill. After all, it is a small thing to forgo in comparison with your wife's comfort.

Don't begin to talk of anything unpleasant while at table. Finish your meal first, and try to banish all worrying thoughts during its progress; otherwise, not only your meal but your wife's will be badly digested.

XI.—CHILDREN.

Don't say anything to your children that may tend in any way to lower their estimation of their mother.

Don't let your wife devote herself so exclusively to the children that you

are left out in the cold. She doesn't
put you there on purpose, but you must
show her that you are still her husband
and lover, and expect to be treated
as such.

Don't think it a nuisance when your
boys or girls want your help in their
studies. Give it to them pleasantly if
you are able to do it at all; if not,
say so.

Don't always say, "Ask your mother,"
when *you* don't want to be bothered.
It is conceivable that *she* doesn't,
either.

Don't say, "That's not in my line,"
when your wife asks your advice about
the children. It *ought* to be in your
line.

Don't say always that you are too tired to play with your children. They want to feel that they have a father as well as a mother.

Don't forget to set an example to your children of being thoughtful for their mother. They will soon learn to save her in all sorts of little ways if they see that *you* always do it.

Don't be unreasonable in your demands on your wife's time during the child-rearing years. If you join her in her hours with the children, you will find added joys in your life, and will not miss her exclusive attentions to you.

Don't leave to your wife everything in connection with the education and upbringing of the children. Discuss all points of difficulty with her, and come to an agreement as to the best way to act under given circumstances.

Don't let your children fear you. Love, not fear, is the key to their characters.

Don't be a wet blanket. In many households all the light - hearted laughter and chatter ceases automatically as soon as father's step is heard. It might have been turned off at the tap, so sudden is the silence. This is all wrong. Your children should feel that you delight in their pleasure.

Don't stick too closely to the old adage that "Children should be seen and not heard." Of course, you must guard against their making nuisances of themselves, especially before visitors. They must learn not to come into the limelight too much, but you don't want to stifle self-expression. Encourage them to speak freely of their ideas.

Originally published 1913

Republished 2007
by A & C Black
Bloomsbury Publishing PLC
50 Bedford Square,
London
WC1B 3DP

www.bloomsbury.com

Bloomsbury is a registered trademark of
Bloomsbury Publishing Plc

ISBN 9780713687910

A CIP catalogue record for this book is available
from the British Library.

Printed by WKT Company Ltd, China